# GROWING OLD

## OLD

*What It's All About*

Diane Livingston, Ph.D.

**BALBOA**.PRESS

A DIVISION OF HAY HOUSE

Balboa Press books may be ordered through booksellers or by contacting:

Balboa Press
A Division of Hay House
1663 Liberty Drive
Bloomington, IN 47403
www.balboapress.com
844-682-1282

Print information available on the last page.

ISBN: 978-1-9822-5284-7 (sc)
ISBN: 978-1-9822-5286-1 (hc)
ISBN: 978-1-9822-5285-4 (e)

Library of Congress Control Number: 2020918924

Balboa Press rev. date: 10/13/2021

*Dedicated to the Hearts and Minds of Elders Everywhere*

# CONTENTS

# INTRODUCTION

## "I Am Not Old Yet!"

*I* WAS OLD BEFORE I became truly curious about it. It's a stage of life, after all, that many Americans have negative ideas about. The associations with aging are so negative that many young people tend to overlook or dismiss old people; and old people often refuse to talk about what aging is really like. So, what is aging like?

That's what I wanted to know—not just from my own experience but from the experience and research of other people. I wanted answers to my many questions because I knew those answers would help me as I continued to age. So, at a time when others might have thought of me as old but I didn't, I set out to learn:

What does it feel like to grow old?

What are the challenges and concerns of this new stage?

What are the possibilities, the virtues, the struggles, and the surprising perks?

Why are we often seen as uninteresting, grumpy, and boring—as somehow less than? And, most poignantly: Why don't we want to talk about it? Why do we try to hide our age, our wrinkles, our sagging skin, our plodding feet? Why do we try to deny to ourselves as well as to others that we are becoming old?

In 2018, there were forty-six million people aged sixty-five or older in the United States. By 2060, it is estimated there will be ninety-eight million![1] That's a lot of Elders! (You'll note I often use the word "Elder" instead of "senior." I believe the term "Elder" bestows more dignity on our aging population that is often deserved but too often not given.) I have also learned that there is not a lot of interest in us from younger people or even some older people. I have learned that few people know who we are, what we do, what we think, or what we feel—even though we can be found almost everywhere if one is looking.

Our stories of aging too often remain hidden because we wear our stories on the inside. As a result, it is easy to misunderstand who we are at this special stage of life, which often leads to isolation and more misunderstanding. But why? We certainly can't avoid it. Can we, instead, make friends with aging, I wondered.

These were some of the driving questions that came alive for me when I was in my late seventies. After a long career as a forensic and clinical psychologist, I retired at sixty-seven and moved to the high mountains of Mexico near the Guatemalan border. Service is one of my strongest values. I soon discovered that indigenous Maya women and children risked their health by breathing in toxic smoke particles while cooking on open fires on dirt floors. Adults and children too often suffered horrific burns from these fires and the deforestation of the forests was inevitable to meet the family's cooking needs. I hoped I could help in some way.

For several years I tried to help by soliciting donations in the United States to support the building of stoves that would meet the specific cooking needs of the Maya culture. The goal of the placement of these stoves was to eliminate the toxic smoke, the burns, and the deforestation of the surrounding forest. With the help of a stove engineer from the Aprovecho Research Center in Oregon, I was able to design a stove that would do just that.

Then, at seventy-nine I returned to the United States to be closer to my children and grandchildren. I moved into an independent living residence for elders in California where I was surprised to see so many old people—but still did not count myself as one of them.

That's when I set out in pursuit of answers to my questions about what it is like to be old. We know that the thoughts and feelings of young people are often about relationships, school, friends, sex, fun, and achievement. And, we know that middle-aged people have thoughts and feelings that generally center around relationships, marriage, child-rearing, responsibilities, earning money, and being successful both inside and outside of the workplace. But what about the thoughts and feelings and the inner lives of Elders here in America as they negotiate the latter stages of life? Instead of growing up, are we now growing down?

❧ ❧ ❧

We can easily imagine that issues of health, relationships, comfort, loss, money, regrets, pain, and sex (yes, even sex!) as well as death and dying are lurking somewhere in the minds and hearts of older adults. But what are some of the perfectly normal thoughts and feelings that most elders carry tucked inside and out of sight: thoughts and feelings that are sad, funny, angry, grateful, wise, or scary?

Today's older generation was raised at a time when people did not usually share personal thoughts and feelings. Common issues like depression, anxiety, regrets, illness, helplessness, physical deterioration, sex, and so on were mostly unspoken. Indeed, we are sometimes criticized for our "organ recitals" about physical changes and complaints that are normal in an aging body.

But there is much more to aging than normal aches and pains in our bodies. The heart and mind can hurt, too. It is important to know that these organ recitals are sometimes indirect expressions of more uncomfortable emotions like fear, anxiety, confusion, and loneliness.

Sharing what is difficult is difficult, no matter what age we find ourselves. And yet, sharing matters. It makes a difference. Mutual sharing of this special experience of aging in America goes a long way toward softening the parts of us that feel alone, misunderstood, and unheard. The worst part of holding the memories is not the pain. It's the loneliness of it. Memories need to be shared. This journey is a new and very unique experience for every one of us. Finding a pair of accepting and understanding ears can make this inevitable journey softer, gentler, and more meaningful.

🦋　🦋　🦋

In my seventies, I had been aware of some of the perks and pleasures of growing old: retirement, sleeping in, having the time and space to enjoy more of life, grandchildren, taking up a new hobby, less pressure, and more freedom. What's not to like? But what, I wondered, really happens at eighty and beyond? Are the alternating fortunes of living and loving so different during this latter stage of life?

I hoped that finding the answers to my questions would give me some sense of control over what lies before us all. I did not want to walk this unclear road completely uninformed. The unknown sometimes makes me uncomfortable.

My search for more understanding about this bumpy but precious journey took me into libraries, senior residences, book stores, assisted living residences, and my own independent residence for Elders. I also attended a Death Cafe to share and to learn about the mysteries of death and dying and how others experience end-of-life issues. Books and journal articles—especially by end-of-life counselors who have sat at the bedside of thousands of dying people and shared publicly the wisdom gathered privately—also added to my understanding of what Elders think and do.

But, eventually, it became clear that I needed to go to the source—Elders themselves—and simply ask: "What does it feel like to grow old?"

I soon learned many people don't want to answer that question. Many people say:

"I'm doing fine, so there is nothing to talk about."

"No one is interested in how I feel."

"It's all downhill for me now, and I don't want to talk about it!"

But I kept at it and eventually I received one hundred and twenty-five responses from men and women ranging from sixty-five to ninety-nine years old. These VOICES ranged from "aging sucks" to "I wouldn't trade this journey for the world." They were sent to me via the internet, Facebook, email, snail-mail, and phone calls; and some were personally handed to me in my senior residential community. Some came in the form of a few words, one sentence, a few paragraphs, or several pages. All openly reflected thoughts and feelings about a subject considered by many too difficult, too confusing, or too scary to discuss. Together, these stories—these VOICES as I think of them—form the beginning of a rich tapestry of what it is like to grow old in America. I bow in gratitude to each and every VOICE found in the pages of this book.

These Voices also form what I consider to be the soul of this small book: a primer about growing old for those of us sixty-five and older, a simple peek into the story of aging. I now have a beginning answer to my original question, "What does it feel like to grow old?" I have also written this book to shine a small light on some of the human issues that will eventually confront all of us as we, too, arrive at these last and inevitable chapters in our life's stories. I hope that this book can make even a small difference in how Elders are perceived in America, both to others as well as to ourselves.

Although meant for an older population, younger souls have much to learn from the experienced voices of Elders who are already walking down this path. Two of my grandchildren told me that this book would have value for them as well, even though it does not apply to their lives right now. So, listen up younger souls! There is so much to learn for all of us, both young and old.

I have personally learned so much on this journey: about growing old, becoming an Elder, and contemplating death and dying. I have learned not only from my readings and the many people who shared their thoughts and feelings but also from living among Elders and, of course, from my own aging experience as well.

So, is it all that bad? No, it isn't! The process of aging is about more than decline. It really is. Contrary to popular opinion, I have learned that we Elders are very interesting people. Many people today judge us by what is on the outside but our stories are on the inside and they are often rich and varied indeed.

I have also learned that there are many pleasures of aging. I love having more time and less responsibility. Like many other grandparents, I experience my grandchildren as a happy addition to this age. There are also the pleasures of just being alive, the opportunities to pursue unmet personal interests, and the pleasure of just hanging out with family and friends, of looking at trees and singing in the rain.

I have also learned that we are better equipped than earlier generations to live life more fully and perhaps longer. Thanks to neuroscience we now know that "...our brains continue to grow into old age!"[2] This exciting information about brain cell birth and death should give us the courage to continue living and loving and growing and learning every day.

Of course, I am also learning that aging is a process that can be both easy and difficult, gentle and bumpy, and sometimes like an untidy ride through the latter chapters of our lives. We also have to admit that to grow old is to live with uncertainty. I wonder: How much time do I have left? Will I die alone? Will I experience pain? Will I be remembered when I am gone?

I have also learned that information, no matter how limited, makes me feel safer as I venture into new territory; and I wanted to share it with you—hoping that you, too would benefit from this information and wisdom as you walk your personal walk down the many different corridors of aging and perhaps beyond.

Do you feel at all anxious about aging? Are you calm and trusting in your beliefs about death and dying? Are you interested in what you, yourself, feel about aging? My older heart would be gladdened if this book proved worthy enough to better serve you about the surprising journey of aging that awaits us all.

# CHAPTER 1

# THE JOURNEY BEGINS

*"Growing older is certain; growing
wiser is harder and optional."*

Debasish Mridha

𝓘 CAN REMEMBER THE day I became "old," at least in
my mind. I was looking in the bathroom mirror
and the face looking back at me was that of an old
woman. I was shocked. I looked at my hands, seemingly for
the first time, and said to the mirror: "These can't be my
hands! These are not my hands!" Woefully, I could say this
about my other body parts but I will spare you the details. I
have always thought of myself as an attractive woman, not
beautiful but attractive enough. But suddenly, I looked like
an old woman.

Jane Fonda once said that old age is "really scary when you
are looking at it from the outside. When you're inside it's not

scary at all. You feel better." I am still learning that there are many reasons why this is sometimes true.

The U.S. Government tells us that sixty-five is the age when we might need help. It is certainly true that it takes more time and energy to keep our many parts up and running. And Medicare is the government's social welfare program to help seniors with the health issues that usually accompany aging folks after sixty-five or so.

Elders in America, as well as some other cultures, are often seen as a growing burden on society. According to Dr. Gordon Livingston, "We are considered to be unproductive, increasingly frail, vulnerable, and more and more dependent. For some, these attributes are considered diseases. The old are stigmatized as infirm in mind and body. Apart from our continuing role as consumers, the idea that old people have anything useful to contribute to society is seldom entertained."[3] Dr. Laura Carstensen observes that the media reflects our collective anxiety about growing older. She calls this the "misery myth."[4]

Yes, we face more limitations, health issues increase, fewer opportunities are open to us, we face loss and discrimination. We are growing closer to death. And, "unfortunately some search for solace in alcohol and drugs."[5]

Just mention the word "aging," and both young and old people alike immediately respond with negative stereotypes about the way we old people look (wrinkled), the way we act (boring), and how frail and burdensome we must be.

No wonder so many of us dread growing old in America. No wonder so many of us lie about our age. My mother never admitted to being more than thirty-nine! But is aging all bad? And what would happen if its positive aspects were valued?

The truth is that there is much more to aging than a downhill spiral. Really! It is not mostly about loss, sadness, depression, pain, anxiety, and fear. It was such a happy surprise for me to realize that oldness is not reflected by the number of years we spend on this planet. One can be young or old at any age.

I believe there would be less decline in both our mental and physical health or at least a slower decline if the American culture viewed its Elders as more worthwhile, competent, and interesting. Put another way, being valued is a very important part of aging well. Knowing that we have something to offer that is held in high regard would be like manna from our culture. We have much to offer, but it is too often not seen and not understood. So, let's draw back the curtain.

As I mentioned in the introduction, there are many pleasures of aging. There is the relief that comes with the freedom that is finally available to many of us from many of life's numerous responsibilities: the joys of grandchildren, the simple pleasures of just being alive, of hanging out with family and friends and puppies, and of sleeping in or staying up late. There is also the opportunity to pursue unmet personal interests, embrace meaningful volunteer opportunities or even become entrepreneurs! More and more Elders do not want to grow old the way their parents did. Many are finding new meaning and purpose in life; a gift that often eluded them in their youth.

Researchers have also found that, in contrast to our drama-filled youth, Elders learn how to "...deal with conflict more effectively and manage their emotions better."[6] This lessens the experience of sadness, anger, and fear. Researchers at the University of Michigan also found that Elders deal with social conflict more effectively than younger people. I know that most of the time I really do feel calmer. And what about you?

I have also gained a perspective on my life that would have not been possible before. As a woman now in my eighth decade, some of the chapters in my story are happy and some are sad. Some involve lonely experiences and some are marked by struggle. Depression, the kind that hurts the heart, crossed my path from time to time, and physical limitations from an accident colored my life with pain for many years. But there are also chapters tinted with enough joy, satisfaction, and even comedy that I rest in gratitude. I like to think that whatever wisdom I have gained on this bumpy ride is because of what I have learned from life's inevitable struggles. But it has taken the distance of many years for me to see the blessings of the darker chapters. I could not see the big picture of my life until now.

Perhaps one of the most compelling pieces of evidence that reveal that aging is far from all bad is this: "Elders often describe the last five or ten years as the happiest years of their lives—an indication of what is known as the Happiness Curve"[7] The Curve looks like this:

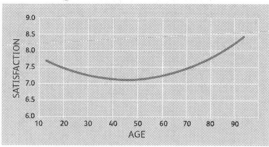

The Happiness Curve is a U-curve that shows that older ages have their challenges. It is true that "…people fear declining health, growing dependence, and increasing isolation. But on average, according to the Happiness Curve, we Elders also count ourselves happier."[8]

Not everyone's life cycles through this U-Curve, but many lives do. Here's the big arc: Life satisfaction seems to take a nosedive around age fifty. It is a time when the pressures of child-raising, work pressures, aging parents, and physical limitations become increasingly real. These burdens usually lift as aging progresses after midlife. Most of us Elders experience an increased freedom in our lives, the kind of freedom that makes it possible to choose to do this and not that, to be here and not there.

In a related study that followed people eighteen to ninety-four over a decade, Dr. Laura Carstensen found that older people "got happier and their emotions bounced around less" than what young people experience.[9]

The Happiness Curve demonstrates that almost forty percent of Americans sixty-five and older rate themselves as very happy but thirty-three percent of Americans aged thirty-five to forty-nine rate themselves as not very happy, according to Robert J. Samuelson.[10] So, be proud and grateful to be old because not everyone makes it to seventy, eighty, or ninety. In my eighties, I know I feel lucky—at least, on the good days.

# VOICES FROM THE FRONT

# What Does It feel Like To Grow Old?

"It happened so quickly I can't believe I'm so old."

Mitzi 86

---

"I'm no longer seen as an important person. It's like I have nothing more to offer."

Paul 80

---

"I feel older when I walk by a mirror and I think it's my mother but it's me."

Tish 76

---

"I used to be able to catch flies with my bare hands. But now I can't even catch the damn things with a fly swatter!"

Carl 86

---

"I plan to return home and maybe find out that I never left. Let me wake up from ignorance and evil. It's time for me to leave. I'm taking up space."

Marisela 95

"I think growing old is a relief of responsibility and accountability. You can just let go and accept life as it now is. When you let go you can experience the peace. You don't have to be brave anymore to anybody. The aches and pains are going to be there. You just have to accept that."

Mark 70

"I fear the dying process and losing my cognitive abilities. I hope I go fast and don't suffer too much. I do believe in an afterlife. I am so curious about it. I have had a full life. I gave birth to six children and they visit often."

Madeline 82

"Screw you. I can finally say whatever I want to say."

Jake 75

"Ridding myself of much of erotic desire and sexual passion has been a huge relief. I also learned that once you listen to others they forget your wrinkles."

Kiki 66

"When I'm gone I want to have used up every asset and body part in His service and afterwards you can throw a party and let the bacteria clean up what is left. This is only the sandbox."

Emily 60

———— ❖ ————

"When I'm sitting down I feel 50 years old. But when I stand up I'm 102."

Mary 89

———— ❖ ————

"I blinked an eye when I was 60 and suddenly I was 91."

Joe 91

———— ❖ ————

"I don't have to shave my legs anymore."

Maryjane 67

———— ❖ ————

"What a delicious relief it is to not have to focus on my appearance like younger people."

Anonymous 89

———— ❖ ————

"There are wonderful things about being 64 and some not so great. I am blessed with a wonderful family that loves me very much. It is the outside world that sees me as an older woman. I feel like a senior and I am invisible sometimes."

Jackie 64

"I am accepting that the body is going to go but the personality and character don't have to."

Sue 76

"When I lie about my age it is in an upward direction. But I don't lie much anymore because what gets better and better as age comes along is grace and character. Of course, it can go the other way but thanks to Jesus, I am still on course and the more grace and character He grows in me, the easier and more fun life and everybody around me becomes, even people who used to drive me nuts!"

Emily 71

"I'm almost 82 and I'm finding the golden years are tarnished. I miss having small children around. I don't have much family nearby and the few that I do have are always busy. I'm fortunate to live in a senior facility and I'm glad to have a roof over my head and other seniors to spend time with but some days are long and lonely."

Joanne 82

"I am aware of my physical losses compared to my earlier age. But I am thankful. I am enjoying growing old. Happy to enjoy life as it shows up."

Art 85

"Everything seems more difficult, even the little things. I am finding it very hard to read. It's not my eyes. It's lack of interest. I just don't care anymore. My heart still leaps up when I see a bunch of violets or pansies. It's like a rainbow, you know. I can't talk today. It's one doctor's appointment after another. If it's not one thing, it's another. I can still enjoy food. People should die before they retire. Who cares what I think!"

Wilma 84

"I now see the beauty all around me that I never noticed when I was young."

Anonymous 76

"At 84 I feel freedom. I am no longer beholden."

AR 84

"I don't care about my wrinkles! Bring 'em on! I have never cared much for fashion, but now that I'm old I can wear what makes me comfy."

Emily 74

"Having a positive attitude and looking at the good things: the ups, not the downs and bad things. It makes a world of difference in life at any age! We all need to be mindful of those things we can be grateful for rather than what we do not have, at any age."

Joyce 75

"It's painful and lonely when your friends begin to die."

Max 88

———— ✳ ————

"It is sometimes hard to remember how precious each day really is; even the difficult days. And yet precious is the right word because everyday is a real gift. Where would we be without it?"

Anne 66

———— ✳ ————

"I'm afraid of being kept alive at any cost."

Anonymous 87

———— ✳ ————

"I know I'm going to hell and I don't care. I don't believe in it."

Anonymous 79

———— ✳ ————

"I've lost my morning bounce. It takes me several hours before I am really up and running again. Ahhh, another loss."

Marylynne 81

———— ✳ ————

"I'm OK with getting old but my body is not."

Anonymous 71

———— ✳ ————

"I don't feel good about myself anymore."

Anonymous 81

"First of all I am not old. I will let you know when I get there. What I am is more vulnerable because my body is aging. This makes me realize how lucky I am to have a partner to share all my joys and tribulations with. Someone I truly love and who loves me. We say that, when it comes to memory, we share one brain between us. Unfortunately, we cannot share bodies. We can only share putting each other back together when we fall or need a new body part. We will see what the future holds."

Tib 84

"I miss my teeth mostly."

Anonymous 99

"Hospice? I don't want to last that long!"

Flossie and Friend 94

"Well, it's quite amusing to me that I still feel young at heart. But when I go doing stuff and being busy, I forget my limitations. For example, I had a couple of bad falls. This made me realize that I had to slow down and look after myself first. About being older, I still ride on my electric bike going too fast. If I don't over do it, I look and feel better. But, yes, some things about growing older are not nice."

Rita 78

"What if I can't take care of myself anymore?"

Anonymous 84

"I am 90 years old and I live in a community that supports my living. There are those that are lively and upbeat. When I wake up each day I try to live each day. I enjoy...being."

Betty 90

"Generally people are not interested in how I feel. I've learned not to say much."

Julia 92

"When I was a kid I wanted to be older...This shit is not what I expected."

Anonymous 81

"Maybe it is because I am hard of hearing but it seems as though people treat me as an invisible person. It's annoying!"

Marilyn 91

"I try to cope with the difficulties of growing old by simply not thinking about it. I also keep busy and read good books."

Helen 90

"Mentally, I'm enjoying the wisdom that comes with age. Physically, I'm afraid there are not as many benefits to growing old."

Jo Jo 69

# CHAPTER 2

# CAN YOU SEE ME NOW?

*"It's not loving a man that makes life harder for gay guys, it's homophobia. It's not the color of their skin that makes life harder for people of color, it's racism. It's not having vaginas that makes life harder for women, it's sexism. And it's ageism far more than the passage of time that makes life harder for all of us."*

Ashton Applewhite
*This Chair Rocks*

*D*EAR ELDER FRIENDS, I have a question for you: Have any of you ever felt invisible? Most older people say that they often feel diminished in American society at large. I too, have felt that way from time to time.

For example, I remember feeling invisible when I was completely ignored during a sidewalk conversation. All the attention was directed to the younger woman at my side as we stood talking to an old male friend of mine. My efforts to participate were mostly ignored. I found that hard to understand; after all, I am quite capable of participating in intelligent conversation. But she was younger and more attractive than I, and that seemed to make all the difference.

And yet, I also remember the first day I arrived at the senior residence where I will most likely spend the rest of my life. I had never spent much time around "old" people like me, and I was filled with uncertainty when I saw so many residents using walkers, wheelchairs, scooters, and canes. These people are really old, I thought. How could I find new friends here? So much oldness! I couldn't see how I could have enough in common with these people. I wasn't that old!

But, of course, I am that old and I am now painfully aware of how very distorted and mistaken my perceptions have been of others aging. Generally speaking we are sometimes considered a burden on society. We are even criticized for using our share of benefits like Social Security and Medicare. Nevertheless, I am hoping that we are being noticed more and more as a potential force of Elders who have something to contribute to society at large. At least being noticed is a start!

As a new resident, it became increasingly clear that I was feeling prejudice against my new friends but I was also feeling prejudice against myself as an old person. Good grief! How interesting that I now see many of these same residents as intelligent, interesting, kind, courageous, and even funny. What changed? It is simply that I now know them. I know some of their stories, and they know some of mine.

Often it's that simple. Knowing someone's personal story changes so much. Sometimes, it changes everything. Of course, we all have some fear in our personal stories—anger, laughter, love, grief, and joy, too. Some of our stories are easier than others. Some are more difficult. But we all have our own unique stories and sharing them removes the sometimes invisible wall that separates us from one another. Sharing a simple two-sentence story can sometimes soften the space between us in a relationship. We find that we can even feel some degree of safety with a stranger. Maybe you have two-sentence stories, too.

I had a similar experience with discrimination when I spent two years working in a maximum-security prison hospital. The patients (all male) were convicted felons. This patient population fascinated me. You might be surprised to learn that it was here that I learned a precious lesson that would serve me for the rest of my life. All of these criminally committed patients were in this hospital to receive an appropriate form of psychotherapy, behavior therapy, and or medication that would hopefully modify their behavior as well as their lack of emotional control and inappropriate ways of thinking.

The lessons I learned were a greater understanding and a deeper sense of compassion. Working with these men allowed me access to their personal stories. It made all the difference. I became less judgmental and more conscious of my own errors in life. Without knowing their stories, I was, like many of you, supportive of locking them up and throwing away the key! Many of you will recognize this common form of discrimination.

But with the knowledge that went beyond their crimes to who they were as individuals, and the experiences and forces that motivated their behavior, I found myself feeling not only understanding but genuine compassion for these men. That doesn't necessarily mean I wanted all of them back on the street—some of them yes, others no. However, it does mean that knowing their stories made it possible for me to see their very real humanness, the sometimes-desperate suffering and cruelty that colored so many of their backgrounds.

None of this is an excuse but cruelty is often the force that makes some people act out their pain. Some of us act out against others in rage, desperation, or fear. Some of us quietly beat ourselves up. And so, on my last day as Clinical Coordinator on my hospital ward, I quietly shed a few tears and said goodbye, feeling gratitude for the very real gift of this experience.

But researchers have found that the most common form of discrimination actually is ageism. Is that why we try to hide our age and the associated ideas that we are grumpy, crotchety, absentminded, forgetful, feeble, a burden, boring, dull, useless, and past our prime?

Our efforts to minimize the outward effects of aging "...fuel a $150-billion-a year cosmetics industry that dwarfs in size other national priorities like education, highway maintenance, or national defense,"[11] We even seem prejudiced against ourselves as well as other older adults. Is it simply because we are afraid? Afraid because the time will come when most of us will eventually live with an increased probability of physical and possible mental limitations? Afraid because we will be seen as "less than?" Afraid that our value will be minimized and we will inevitably be ostracized because we are old? Is that why Elders hide their age when they should be flaunting it?

Do I feel less valued when I step out into a society that is much larger and diverse than the retirement home where I live? Yes, I do, a little. I agree that the life I am living as an older person has become smaller and more contracted and a little more dependent but, at 80-plus years old, it is a comfortable change for me. What is uncomfortable is that I have slowly learned, that in general, we Elders are often seen as uninteresting, dull, slow, cranky, unattractive, sexless, etc., and without value. Really? Yes, really! But why? Because we are old!

Ashton Applewhite and other researchers have written about the similarity of sexism and racism to ageism. I agree with them. Ageism is just as prevalent, and just as ignored. "Our society devalues old age in many ways and this is particularly true in America where individualism, self-reliance, and independence are so highly valued, perhaps overly valued."[12] We forget that respect, cooperation, and working together are essential counterparts for a healthy and productive society.

I, and Elders in general, often receive help when we are out and about and alone. I am frequently helped by a younger person when carrying a large package, walking on hilly terrain, and so on. Maybe it is simply because I use a cane when walking outside. I love this kind of thoughtful contact with strangers. It always leaves a warm touch on my heart. I wonder how often you, dear readers, have also received such friendly gestures of help.

Unfortunately, these acts of kindness are not enough to reduce the impact that discrimination plays in our everyday lives. "Society has tended to overlook, undervalue, and stereotype the elderly and that this stereotype is often based on myths and assumptions."[13] Instead of respect or reverence, we Elders are also more likely to be seen as a burden on society and even invisible! To make matters worse, women are perceived as old before men are and therefore devalued more and earlier! But we knew that, didn't we? Surely ageism is something we can change.

Have you noticed how under-represented Elders are in so many aspects of our lives? I am so accustomed to seeing only young or middle-aged people on TV, I no longer notice that we Elders are not only under-represented but often not represented at all. The exception is in advertising that now targets the age-specific needs of our older population. We have become worthy consumers with purchasing power! But as public faces, we remain very much on the sidelines. We have to ask ourselves why this is so when approximately forty-six million Elders are living in the United States today!

Research clearly shows that prejudice and discrimination against older adults are woven into the fabric of American culture. Because so many of us deny and try to hide the fact that we are growing older and older, we feed the prejudice we know so well.

Discrimination against Elders can also be very costly. Research shows that stereotyping of Elders negatively impacts housing opportunities because we are not always seen as reliable renters. We might be a nuisance! We might die! We might run out of money! This is true even though prejudice against older people around housing and rental issues is illegal. Elders also shoulder concerns about the possibility of being evicted due to health problems, accessibility issues, mental health issues, handicapped problems, etc., all of which create housing problems not usually faced by younger souls.

More and more Americans also believe they are facing age-based discrimination at the office. "Nearly two in three workers ages forty-five to seventy-four said they have seen or experienced age discrimination in the workplace. Of those, a whopping ninety-two percent say it was very or somewhat common. Facebook, Yahoo, Google, and Twitter have all been accused of age discrimination."[14]

Also, our job possibilities are limited because younger people often begin employment with smaller salaries. This makes it harder for higher paid Elders to hold on to their jobs. In addition, we older workers are not as skilled in newer technical innovations. As a result long term job security has become a thing of the past.

It seems that there also needs to be more conversation in our federal government about the opportunities and needs for various kinds of volunteer services that could be happily and productively filled by retired Elders. Wouldn't this financial contribution offset some of the costs of Social Security and Medicare? Wouldn't this financial contribution help reduce the frequency of complaints that we retired folks are a drain on social services? "Discrimination due to age is one of the great tragedies of modern life. The desire to work and be useful is what makes life worth living, and to be told your efforts are not needed because you are the wrong age is a crime."[15]

Ashton Applewhite tells us that "...discrimination against Elders can even be found in healthcare when we are occasionally passed over for some surgical procedures because it is thought that we won't benefit that much, and we won't be around long enough to make good use of the investment of medical skill and money." She also tells us that "...in intensive care units, younger patients sometimes receive more aggressive treatment to save functioning and life than older patients receive."[16]

We do not need medical ageism. But it exists. Ageism in healthcare is real. Geriatric doctors site other medical doctors who belittle gerontology, the medical profession that specializes in the evaluation and treatment of older adults. These geriatric doctors also speak of "...over treatment, under treatment, and talking down to older patients. This is, of course, demeaning, disrespectful and can lower self-esteem and depression in older patients."[17]

Fewer physicians choose gerontology as a specialty because the pay is lower, and the professional status is lower than in other medical specialties. Drs. Karin Ouchida and Mark Lachs cite the many ways that this is so. For example, "It is under treatment when, without investigation, bruises in an elderly patient are dismissed as the normal effects of anticoagulants, not the result of family violence. The failure to treat problems, such as erectile dysfunction or sexually transmitted diseases, is because doctors simply assume that their older patients are not sexually active is another example. Some Elders present with headaches, confusion, and or memory loss but no tests to rule out a possible brain tumor are ordered because of the age discrimination belief that these symptoms were just a normal part of aging."[18]

Over treatment also exists. "When doctors prescribe medications but do not take into consideration important factors such as age, personal preferences, specific abilities, and the general ability to function in their lives, important information is lost. The prescribed medications might not be as appropriate and might even do harm."[19] Add the potential harm from some drug interactions and one wonders how the medical care of Elders will be comprised during this most difficult of pandemics: Covid-19. After all, in the eyes of society, we are probably considered the most expendable of patients. It is abundantly clear that Elders do not always receive the care they want, need, and deserve.

Be honest with yourselves. Don't you too harbor some prejudice against Elders? I am embarrassed to tell you that sometimes I am prejudiced against you and against me, too.

Discrimination against Elders can be found all around the world. This kind of prejudice is sometimes deeply ingrained and found more frequently in western cultures. In other countries, discrimination against the elderly, when it exists, is often softened by cultural respect felt toward the long-lived members of a group.

When the Peace Corps was established in 1961 under President Kennedy, if I had not been married with small children, I would have been the first to sign up. When I retired at age sixty-seven, I searched for a place where I could live out my dream that involved serving those less fortunate than me. In the mountains of Chiapas, Mexico, I found the poorest state in Mexico with the largest indigenous population and it called to me. I ended up living and working there for almost ten years. In the Mexican cities and the indigenous Maya communities, I was respected simply because I was an Elder, and I was called Doña Diana. Older men received the prefix Don so Francisco became Don Francisco.

Some cultures revere their Elders and confer names and titles on them that confer respect for a life long-lived. In India, for example, the suffix "ji" is used after a name so that Ajooni becomes Ajooniji. "Mzee" before a name is used in parts of Africa to demonstrate respect for the experience and knowledge of an elder. Kolawole becomes Mzee Kolawole.

A Guatemalan proverb tells us that "Everyone is the age of their heart." There is also a wonderful African proverb that says: "When an Elder dies, an entire library burns down." It does! The loss of life experience and life teachings are huge. How different these perspectives are when compared to our American culture.

American culture is more focused on the age of our bodies and does not acknowledge that, in general, Elders in America are sitting on piles of uncovered knowledge found in both the body, the heart, and the mind. Oh, what stories and accomplishments American Elders could tell.

In America, however, there is no special gesture of respect for all the many chapters that define the stories of older people in our culture. Mrs., Mr., or Ms. are as close as we come to conferring respect for a life long-lived and even these common words are not commonly used anymore.

What makes one culture respectful and caring of its older citizens while, for example, our own culture idolizes the outer beauty of youth? There is such a misguided obsession with youth in America that hurts younger people as well as older people. The superficial values learned from powerful and relentless advertising shapes a value system that does not serve Elders and affects our impressionable young people. A great deal of money is made off of our children using commercial manipulation aimed at convincing them that they need this and must have that, whether or not they or their families have the money to pay for it. Does this serve the real needs of our children? And, when our young people have learned to want but can't always have, they often feel "less than." Do we really want this for our children?

How has our American culture learned to see our Elders in such a negative light? How is the dignity for older people expressed or more commonly not expressed? Why can't we see that "As we grow old, the beauty steals within."[20] In American culture, one simply has to look a little harder for it because this kind of beauty is earned year by year by year and runs deeper than the sexualized and material beauty that defines so much of western culture.

We too, have learned these same distorted perceptions of Elders from families and friends, through television, magazines, books, and through the values we live by and the people with whom we share our lives. Again, I am guilty. Advertising campaigns are now targeting Elders since we too, have become consumers in ever-growing numbers. But even younger Elders are sometimes portrayed as physically, mentally, and psychologically diminished on television and in movies and magazines.

The good news is that there are exceptions to how Elders are viewed in our American culture. The many grandparents who give of themselves to their grandchildren shape a different and more positive view of older people. Positive and personal contact from a child's grandparents can serve to soften the external perceptions of aging adults.

This was certainly true of my maternal grandmother. We called her Mum Mum and the positive effect she had on my life just by sometimes being there cannot be measured. Unfortunately, most negative perceptions of older people that begin in childhood still tend to remain throughout adulthood. Surely this kind of ageism is something we can change.

# VOICES FROM THE FRONT

# What Does It Feel Like To Grow Old?

"I miss being touched."

Janet 78

"I am trying to figure out how to navigate these next years. It is challenging. My knees are my biggest single physical issue and I am trying to not become distressed as they make my walking more difficult. I look and feel very old when I am moving about here in my home and when I am out in the bigger world. My general appearance is quite deceiving as I know I look younger than my years. I get compliments, of course, but the truth is when I walk I feel like I am 97 not 87! I am truly not afraid of dying but of course want it to be pain free and with my brain intact."

Mitzi 88

"Aging sucks!"

Mary 74

"Growing old has been difficult for me. At first, after retirement, I had difficulty with no longer having work as part of my identity. I spent time with the question, 'Who am I?' Also I began to experience limitations. Multi-tasking became difficult, my exercise routine had to be modulated, my short term memory developed holes. I initially found myself trying to be as I had been. I foolishly took on tasks I could no longer handle and became ill. Gradually, with time, I have come to accept my aging as part of my life…Now as I deal with my infirmities and their ongoing need for care, I live with my husband (2nd time around-married 40 years) in an independent housing hotel with 45 other people who, for the most part, are kind and have a good sense of humor. I am involved in many activities with yoga, a writing group, and musical events to scrabble with my daughter who lives nearby. At present, I feel as if I have a vibrant and satisfying life. I treasure each day for I do not know how much more time I have left. What I do know is that I have been lucky."

Barbara 78

"As we get older body parts start wearing out but we just go on because it most definitely beats the alternative of Not Getting Older. The cruelest thing is when the mind goes. That hasn't happened to me yet, thank God! I have some serious life-altering issues but thankfully no life-threatening issues at this point."

Sam 85

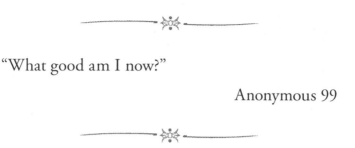

"What good am I now?"

Anonymous 99

"I'm sure as hell not invisible here. Everyone knows me all over. The other day I rode by a crowd of motorcycle lovers. I am on my ATV. They all cheered! What a rush! Fun! 71 is still OK."

Judy 71

"I am currently going through an exercise found in Stephen Levine's book called *A Year to Live*. I am living this year like it was my last. The exercise includes facing Death and the idea of Death, squarely. The book suggests that we explore any fears we have around Death then to examine these fears, look through them, lean into them and eventually embrace the idea of Death. I have done this, and I will do it again."

Robert 62

"I have had a very satisfying life. And now in my seventies I feel happy and relaxed. I am aware that time has shifted for me and that is a good thing overall. My schedule doesn't stress me. I can fit in all the things I loved and missed out on during earlier chapters. I have a small rural cabin, a barn, pasture for a horse and mule and room for 3 dogs and a cat. I am comfortable with myself and have time for friends, fun, and as much work as I want. This can be a very good time and I hope to keep this pattern...and adjust my time when needed. It is good to watch loose ends tie together as earlier interests find outlets and unanswered questions find answers. This is a good time."

Dee 70

"It seems people define others by a preconceived idea of numbers of what another must be like if they reach a certain number. Very annoying."

Ruth 85

"At 83 I realize more and more each day how blessed I am to have been born white in this country. May the day come soon when color will no longer be an issue. I also know now that a loving family is the greatest gift we can be given or for us to give. I was blessed."

Kaki 83

"Things keep getting scarier. There is so much unknown in growing old. First there was the loss of my parents years ago and I know there will be time when my children too, will be parentless and I know the pain of that loss. By the time I reached my seventies I had to make an adjustment to living in this new body. I still think I can just get up and go but my body requires a transition before I can even move. My heart is heavy as each of my friends are struggling with their physical and mental issues. There use to be a day when I wondered whose wedding I would be attending next and then it was the weddings of my children and their friends. Now I wonder whose funeral I will be attending and who will be left to attend mine and how my life will come to an end. It's a balance now of losses and blessings."

Gidge 77

"Growing older, no matter the starting point, there is always room for the unexpected. I am now 81 and not a year goes by that I am not surprised by life itself. Never a dull moment if you are awake to life. And life? Sometimes good and sometimes not good at all."

Ben 70

"I'm still working, still teaching scuba diving, still swimming in the bay, not at all ready to throw in the sponge, yet surprised by, and thankful for my energy and mobility. Fast forward another 17 years, having reinvented myself as a Certified Residential Real Estate Appraiser, and then becoming a Longshoreman. Signs of aging are now beginning to appear. Most of these signs of the onset of fragility are my own fault. More exercise and stretching would help. Still, having broken most of life's rules, having done nothing to earn my longevity, I find myself alive and well and enjoying life in spite of myself. WOW! Hard to believe!"

Harrison 82

"I became 75 on my last birthday. Lots of things are better but physical stuff not as good; less energy, sciatica, arthritis, etc. Oh well, Esta La Vida."

Ruth 75

"Everything seems more difficult – even the little things."

Anonymous 82

"I feel great! I've paid my dues."

Joe 90

"The older I become, it becomes increasingly difficult to find heroes."

Rita 65

"When I was in my teens, it seemed to me and my age mates that it was more desirable to be an adult and to be able to do whatever you wanted, that I wasted a lot of time wanting to be older than I was. Later I realized that it was a big mistake to wish your life away, and I am determined that I would never waste time in my old age wanting to be younger than I am. As a result, I am contented to be old. I am fortunate I have good health so far, and not in pain with arthritis, as so many are. I enjoy what I do and make a practice of being grateful for the many blessings in my life. Having dear friends and a loving family is such good fortune. I still enjoy learning and think that is one of the secrets of remaining young at heart."

Meghan 91

"I have had innumerable requests for the secret to my long life. First, have a sense of humor. Exercise is very important. Just say to yourself, 'Life is sweet.' This is sage advice."

Rita 99

"As I have grown older my memories of past events are slipping away as I now focus on living in the present — a gift to appreciate each day. However, I find it more difficult to accomplish the normal activities of each day accomplishing less and less each day. It's rather demeaning but I must accept reality. This old gal ain't what she used to be. Other than that, I'm glad to still be alive under any circumstances."

Norma 94

"By my mid-seventies, work was finished, kids were grown and married, and a new love and life for me. New hips, new lenses, numerous medications, grandchildren, a second major relocation, more doubles than singles in tennis, the end of sailing and more frequent naps all contributed to my new reality. At 81, I am old!"

Dudley 81

"I live at the 'the home' now that I'm old. I can't really believe that I'm here. Where did all my 'stuff' go, all those items so dear, that someone loves them like I did, I do hope to hear. It is hard to let go of all that is so dear."

Natalie 92

"Much that happens comes to us by chance over which we have little or no control. Shakespeare spoke of the slings and arrows of outrageous fortune and we are all subject to them, some more and some less."

Loren 82

"There are many delightful children who cannot stand growing up, they come to nothing, and in the same way later in life there are many people who cannot endure age — the good qualities disappear and nothing comes to replace them. It is as if they mostly fade, without maturing. I have actually thought (often) about this: how age is the greatest test for everyone-just as with good wine, 'It takes a really good vintage to stand up to long keeping.' From Isak Dinesen's Letters from Africa Ngong. Mom 9iv 23"

Meghan 94

"Aging makes us all sooner or later fragile, vulnerable, and dependent on others. I try to pretend to be more capable and independent than I really am and that masquerade also becomes a burden and a daily stress. But it is too hard to come out of the closet and just show myself as old and blinder by the day and ask for help!"

Kiki 69

"The other day an older friend told me about her very young relative who loves to talk to her and does not ignore her because she is old. Very often old people are ignored because of their advanced age. They have to live a life where, maybe, the material comforts are looked after, but not their emotional needs."

Lakshmi 75

"Getting old is a state of mind. Now I am 91. I'm badly crippled, but I still think I'm 15."

Flossie 91

"We have seen a lot, done much, struggled, watched as technology stole our contact with each other and our children and grandchildren. No longer thoughts about a phone call, a note, or a picture you can hold in your hand. I once heard a young neighbor say about my other neighbor who was 89, 'I don't go to see her because she starts crying.' Everyone she knew was gone or moved away. Her three daughters only come on holidays. It will be their time soon to find out why old people cry."

Barbara 77

"I love getting older. My understanding deepens. I can see what connects. I can weave stores of experience and apply them. I can integrate the lessons. Things simply become more and more fascinating. Beauty reveals itself in thousands of forms."

Victoria 79

"If old means what I suppose it means, then I don't think I am old. Like everyone, I evolved gradually through life's stages and I'm still seeing some things differently than before, still enjoying new experiences. As always there are ups and downs. I plough through the downs and love the ups and live in the here and now."

Judy 90

"Sometimes I forget that I have grey hair and that I'm not 15 years old anymore. Darn it! Staying young at heart is so important just as feeling appreciated is."

Angie 69

"I am afraid to die."

Jenny 81

"Life is hard and death is too."

Bob 90

"For the first time in my life I have time to do all the things I couldn't do before."

Anonymous 71

"I have lost more and more contact with people as I grow older. Often they are no longer here. The loss of my husband of 61 years was very, very hard. Being old is lonely."

Anita 94

"Part of living is getting older. As it progresses you must get bolder. Smile as you age, pretend you are a sage, let the younger ones lean on your shoulder."

Sarah 85

"I guess we all feel young until the body starts failing."

Janet 70

"Absence for many retirees does not make the heart grow fonder. Geography takes the zip out of just being there in person. Sadly, some of my dearest friends have died. Others are not as diligent about staying in touch. New connections at my age are very difficult to make. Making new friends takes energy, time, and commitment. I urge all of you who are growing old to make sure you guard against this loss if connections are important to you."

Dudley 81

"This month, as I join my husband in the illustrious company of octogenarians, I'm surprised we've come so far and still with all our original parts intact. Remembering my mother's words that health ranks higher than wealth or any other of life's gifts. I heartily agree that we have only one body to be treasured and tenderly treated. That goes for our minds which thrive on exercise as well...since we only go through this life once. I insist on living to the fullest while encountering energy limitation that feel somehow alien. So, there will be re-calculations along the way. Aging is about losses and discoveries, too... Finally, as an immigrant, this journey of aging has been humbling, amazing, rewarding, with adventure in a country rich and powerful. Each day we have the freedom to give and receive LOVE, the currency of our humanity. We are wisdom wealthy, and I'm proudly grateful for friends, family, and mentors who have been here, leading, guiding, lifting, supporting, and smoothing the bumps."

Katie 80

# CHAPTER 3

# THE ROAD WELL TRAVELED

*"Life should not be a journey to the grave with the intention of arriving safely in a pretty and well-preserved body, but rather to skid in broadside in a cloud of smoke, thoroughly used up, totally worn out, and loudly proclaiming "Wow! What a Ride!"*

Hunter S. Thompson

W E DON'T GROW old overnight, thank goodness! But we do seem to grow old by stages all through our lives. I am eighty plus years old but feel, relatively speaking, somewhat young inside. My health is still good, so far. Not great but could be worse. Oh, there are days when I feel at least ninety but I try to be grateful for these days as well. I can always take a nap! And occasionally, I still have a wonderful soaring moment when it feels like God is in the heavens and all is right with the world. Gratitude can come more easily as we age, and we can wear life more lightly.

Happily, what is more and more true for many of us as we age is that we feel we have more freedom to be more of who we really are. Often our more authentic selves have been hidden in our earlier years underneath the burden of everyday living. "To be ourselves in a world that is constantly trying to make us someone else, is the greatest accomplishment."[21] This is hard work! However, with advancing years, the pressure on our younger selves to conform to the dictates of our culture begins to soften. What a relief!

Perhaps this is why we find so much more uniqueness among us as Elders. We have the freedom to be more authentic, more our true selves. It's like coming home to ourselves in ways we couldn't before and it feels good. Our unconscious usually directs us to be this way and not that way, for us to do this instead of that, throughout our lives. But as we age we are more likely to loosen these social constraints that have kept us in our place for millennia.

This first or early stage of our oldness is often called Elderhood. It happens when we are around sixty-five or so, and it is rich with opportunities that are not available to us at younger ages. Some call it the Golden Years. If our circumstances are such that we are graced with our basic needs for food, shelter, clothing, and protection, as well as family, friends, and reasonably good health, our journey continues with new possibilities. However, if our basic human needs and positive contact with other people are not met, the journey to and through the stages of Elderhood can be very difficult indeed.

🦋　🦋　🦋

During the early years of growing old, a caring compassion seems to emerge for many of us and involves a significant desire to "give" in some way. Have you noticed that? Have you tried "giving" to others in some meaningful way? Often the key to a meaningful life is to embrace acts of kindness, to help those in need, in whatever manner fits us. We know that giving of ourselves to others enhances the life of the "giver" as long as our motive is simply to give and not to give in order to get something in return. Genuine giving is its own reward.

I challenge all of us, myself included, to search for a "Giver" waiting to be discovered in our hearts. If uncertainty resides there, find a way to do it anyway! Having a purpose that is larger than ourselves can change our lives as well as the lives around us at any stage. My years with the Maya in Mexico met my long-held need to find purpose outside of the more conventional life that I had established for myself, no matter that I was seventy-something at the time.

Giving to oneself counts too: let the artist within you arise and bloom; country dance and let your spirit feel the joy of happy movement; delight in assisting in your grandchild's classroom; create a fundraising organization; become the bridge player you always wanted to be; or take up meditation. These suggestions are only a few of the many possibilities that await you. Most importantly, simply have some fun.

Dudley Tower, Ph.D.[22] believes that human beings were not meant to retire. Now that's a new idea! And, since the data show us that current life expectancies are close to eighty years old and climbing, we might have twenty to thirty more years after retirement to embrace this later stage of Elderhood. So, engage in a new life. Write a book! Explore latent talents! Save the world! "Find a way to make music with whatever you have left."[23] You'll be so glad you did.

Of course, these late-life opportunities are optional, and we can either embrace them or toss them aside. There is no judgment here. Some of us will continue to strive for a sought-after achievement. Others will embrace a somewhat stress-free style and will choose to relax, sleep in, and listen to the magic of birdsong. Think rocking chair. Think friends. Think chess. Think nature walks. Think music. They each have their advantages.

Have you noticed that it is more and more clear that what we pursue and value most at this stage of aging is an increase in the importance of each moment, the value of each loved one, each sunset, each bird on the wing, each song, each fallen leaf, each human touch. Many of us will be inspired to find a lifestyle that allows us to experience more of these moments.

In the book *The Elder*,[24] "We learn early-stage Elders still have the energy and potential to turn losses into gains." That is, we can still turn around a stumbling block: We can heal relationships, learn forgiveness, make peace with a painful mistake, let go of whatever has made our hearts tight. And, we get to choose. There is no judgment at all for any of these choices.

My dear mother always seemed to want to die relatively early and her unhappiness over her dream-lost life surely made that possible. She just wanted to give up. Her life was a tragedy for those who knew her. I still feel the sadness of knowing who she might have been had she had the necessary support of our culture and opportunities that were simply not available to her. She didn't fit the mold of women in the 1930s, 40s, and 50s. She was a woman, and that fact alone made everything harder, significantly limiting her options in life. There were so many real roadblocks, often unconscious, for girls and women during this era in our country. It was quite acceptable to limit what girls could do if they wanted to work outside the home: teacher, nurse, or secretary were common choices. This was a major limitation but was usually never questioned, even by the women themselves. I, myself, accepted all of this. Hard to believe this in retrospect, but it is true. Add the perceived disgrace of my mother's divorce and it is easy to understand how very stifling this cultural dictate of acceptable roles was for women and girls not so long ago.

You can count me in here as well as I too bought into the erroneous belief that I had limited choices: Wife and motherhood trumped any dreams and was expected for all good girls. If dreams did come true, they did not come true easily and were usually few and far between. How fortunate that times have changed rather drastically, and women now have much more freedom to pursue their personal choices. I got a late start but even with a late start one can re-fashion one's life. I did. It was difficult but worth it.

I must admit that I still harbor some resentments about the discrimination against women that certainly affected my life as a girl growing up in the 1950s. Happily, I can now say that I have healed this resentment. If I had not, I could expect this negative energy to impact my life in any number of unhappy ways, including the shortening of my days on this earth: my days with my dear family and friends, my days with music, nature, and the simple joy of being alive.

I am now proud of my eighty-plus years! I am grateful that I have been able to come this far. But the reality is that if we are fortunate enough to grow as old as I am, most of us will eventually experience increasing dependence on others for basic requirements that include driving, shopping, cleaning the house, medications, and even bathing and dressing, etc. If we are lucky, and too many of us are not, we will exist safely in our own homes, living alone or with friends or relatives. What a happy surprise to learn that approximately five percent of Elders are living in nursing homes with all the limitations that are part of that experience. That means that "ninety-five percent of us can choose to live independently in our family homes, in an independent living retirement home, in a downsized apartment, with extended family, or we can join economic forces with a friend".[25]

I remember when, in a hospital committee meeting some years ago, a geriatric physician drew a red line on the whiteboard. That line illustrated the following: When we Elders have a bad fall, a serious injury, or get very sick, even though we recover, we usually do not recover to the same level of health we had before. That red line, one's individual baseline, usually gets lowered permanently.

Even after all these years, I vividly remember the medical message that was demonstrated by that red line. As my body continues to change and I continue to age, I hope, no I pray, that that red line remains at a reasonably high level in my future.

But eventually the inevitable and growing numbers of our years will take its toll on our physical and perhaps our mental abilities as well, but who knows. That red line has a mind of its own.

As we age, the fullness of our individual stories continues through the next stage — mostly unknown to others. Energy levels usually slow down. Limited activity makes it more difficult to profit from exercise, but not impossible. Walkers, canes, scooters, and wheelchairs limit our speed through life, but do not have to stop us. We often take lovely naps. When we Elders get excited we can still jump up and down on the inside, not so easily on the outside. I must also admit that I am not as energized by social contact even though social contact is paramount in the lives of most Elders and is still important to me. The changing needs of our bodies begin to take center stage.

We might struggle with common memory problems like putting the keys in the refrigerator or forgetting nouns as I do. My organizational skills with paperwork issues like bills, research, communications, etc., no longer feel sharp and clear. Because my ability to organize ideas and information had weakened, writing this book was more difficult for me and took much more time than I anticipated. I simply felt confused from time to time and considered tossing these pages into the trash can. It was just too hard.

But many Elders have only minor problems with memory and organization. I feel envious. I love the response from Mark, my son-in-law, when I announced to my family that my relationship with nouns was changing—I was having trouble finding them! What was her name? What do you call that? What did she buy? Where did he go? I often know the correct answer, but I can't pull it up. My son in law's response to my failing nouns was: "Have you tried verbs, Diane? Verbs are nice." I love this!

Because I live in a residential home for independent Elders, I am learning firsthand about some aspects of life's later stages. I am learning that even with all basic needs met and family members living close by, our latter days can be a challenge. Assisted living or a nursing home might eventually be a necessary next step for some of us. The need for help with bathing and dressing and shopping can often feel like an unwanted intrusion into our personal lives. But it can also feel like a relief when this help is what we want and need.

Alas, I am growing old! I find it difficult to say this. But increasing health problems and decreasing energy levels make it impossible to avoid what is true. Yes, I now plod slowly into the new of each day instead of actively embracing it from the start. It's also true that it now takes twice as much time to do half as much of just about anything. But I am still here doing what I can do, and feel so much more grateful than sad. I am in the process of accepting this new reality, and I must admit acceptance feels a lot better than denial or avoidance. I can even admit that I often prefer spoons to forks! Much easier, less messy. I count my blessings. Life is good. So far.

Time marches on and most of us gradually begin to feel the unwinding of our lives as we have known them. I have been diagnosed with several medical problems because "Things fall apart. The center does not hold."[26] Pastor Gregory Rapp clarifies that point with these examples: "Clean things get dirty. Relationships rust without care. We have to keep oiling the machine and winding the clock. The fit get flabby, and eventually we all wear out, too."[27] For thousands of years, Buddhism has stressed the impermanence of all things both seen and unseen. And yes, even stars die! Nothing, absolutely nothing, lasts forever. Everything on the face of the earth and beyond eventually perishes and is gone. To think otherwise is pure folly. Our time is limited. Use it wisely!

Although I struggle with some medical problems, this is not what I was expecting. I find it helpful to remind myself that there still is so much that is good in my life and for that I am grateful. Listen to the accumulated wisdom of Helen Keller as she tells us: "I cannot do everything but I can do something."[28] Yes, I too can do something! And I will do as much as I can. Hopefully!

As we Elders continue our journey through life, it is not unusual to feel a mixture of gratitude for the good mixed with fear and uncertainty for the not so good. The path ahead is changing and is not as clear as it used to be.

No matter how hard I try, I am much less productive than I used to be. I like being productive so I count this as another loss but one that I can live with and still be happy. But, a loss here, a gain there. So far, not too bad. Not too bad at all. Although, writing this book has been a struggle because of waning physical energy, mental lethargy, and sometimes confusion, I have not wanted to give up—as tempting as giving up has seemed at times. I drag my feet here because my mind does not do my bidding as it once did. But I really can do something even though I cannot do everything! I don't want to forget this. Thank you Helen Keller for reminding me. I need to remember this over and over and over again.

By now, most of us on our aging journey benefit from various medications, and some of us meditate or do yoga as well. Common cognitive issues like memory problems appear like my trouble finding nouns or leaving papers in unusual places. For some of us, more serious memory problems can significantly impact our lives. Issues like confusion, anxiety, and depression surface. Mental health professionals are available and can often help us through psychotherapy and or medications. But instead we keep busy, more or less, and watch too much TV.

There are many ways to think about these latter life stages but I chose the stages that Dr. Verne Wheelwright has clarified.[29] His stages make common sense to me and are simple, clear, and easy to use. See if you can find yourself in the following simplified Life Stages:

> Stage 1: "Aging and lifestyle changes begin to appear around the age of sixty more or less. Most of us are free of any serious health problems. We are *Independent* and enjoy the freedom that this stage brings."

Stage 2: "Health problems and the need for medications begin to appear for some of us. Although we are more *Vulnerable*, we continue to live our lives with only limited help from family, friends, and the medical profession. We might take a variety of medications." But losses do grow as cognitive problems sometimes loom larger and sometimes, but not always, dominate our lives. However, for the most part, we are free to live our lives with only limited help. The arrival of the Corona Virus increased the vulnerability of us as Elders. Our more advanced age includes more serious medical issues and these medical issues weaken our ability to fight this horrible pandemic. Our choices as to where and how we die are more limited.

Stage 3: "When multiple health problems and cognitive issues begin, so does frailty and the need for assistance with daily self- care. We are *Dependent* as losses continue to grow. An assisted living facility, home health care, or a nursing home might be necessary for some of us." We have to give up some or all of our beloved freedoms including cooking for ourselves, shopping, managing our accounts, etc. Most of us will lose the ability and legal right to drive a car to wherever we choose: to pick up a grandchild after school, spontaneously run errands, visit a friend in a nearby city. Even though there are a growing number of older Elders who do continue to drive, most of us will give up this cherished freedom.

Stage 4: "At this stage, many of us are often faced with multiple health problems. You might say that this is a common consequence of living into our eighties, nineties and beyond. We are not built to live forever. So eventually, when we are faced with multiple health problems, a terminal disease, or the terminal stage of an accident or injury, we are often, but not always, confined to a hospital or a medical facility like an assisted living facility or a nursing home." But I hope this is not me. However, ready or not, this is a transitional time, a fading time, a time with some degree of frailty, and our personal choices dwindle even more. I admit that includes me, too. What is true is that this personal slide toward the end of our final chapter in life is a mystery, a mystery I wish I understood.

During this waning stage of aging, or the end stage of some disease or injury, *End of Life* concerns surface; This is a "time period when health care providers would not be surprised if death occurred within about six months."[30]

Dr. Wheelwright's stages are, of course, oversimplified but I believe they help to clarify a complex subject. These four stages are a good general description of what happens as we age our way through these later years, each in his or her own unique way.

An important reality is that sometimes we may move back and forth within these stages. I started writing this book when I was in Stage 2 and enjoying my Golden Years in my seventies. But when some medical issues challenged my health, I found myself slipping into Stage 3 for some time.

This rendered my life much smaller indeed. I withdrew from a more active lifestyle with the hope that in time I could return to a quiet but more active level of Stage 2. As I write this, I am very much hoping that I can return to what I know and what I was able to do. But will that be possible? Will that somewhat scary red line hover closer to Stage 2 or will I remain in Stage 3, or even Stage 4 till the end? Right now, I don't know. I just don't know.

Of course, Stages 1 and 2 of Elderhood cannot continue forever, nor can we. Many of us will become more vulnerable in heart, mind, and body. Frailty of our bodies and or minds sometimes demand major changes in our choices of what we can and cannot do. I have had to limit my exercise. I count this as a loss for me. Fatigue limits how actively I live my life. At these declining stages, physical and cognitive problems might loom larger and even dominate our lives. Limitations increasingly influence our choices and many of us begin to lose the cherished freedom that we experienced as Elders in Stage 1 and 2.

With the loss of freedom, there is more dependence on resources outside of ourselves. This is hard for me to imagine, because independence has been my way of life. I am concerned and even afraid of this. Sleep, a crucial part of any good day, no longer comes easily for many of us and is no longer as satisfying as it was for me once upon a time. Out of desperation, I have begun taking cannabis for sleep.

It works, and I am grateful. I wish all the problems of aging were as easy to remedy. But I'll take what I can get.

Even though Dr. Wheelwright's Stage Theory seems to be a good description of what happens as we age our way through life, there's more. As we live through every stage of our lives, we have choices, no matter how small. They may be difficult choices—but they are choices—and these choices continue for most of us, most of the time, even if we feel helpless. For example, how we think about the stages of aging is a choice and plays an important role in how we experience these stages. In fact, how we think about aging influences how we feel about it and, ultimately, what we do about it. For example, if you think being "old" means you are helpless, you will likely feel helpless and, yes, act helpless. On the other hand if you think that being "old" means you may have some limitations but you are also capable of many things, you will feel more capable and act on these many things. We do not have to believe what we think.

Many of us engage in distorted thinking—that is, we have irrational thoughts, untrue thoughts, or dysfunctional thoughts—from time to time. But instead of clinging to distorted thoughts that work against us and sometimes wound us, we can choose mentally healthy thoughts that can create new and surprising feelings and behaviors that enhance our lives. Does changing our thoughts make everything all right? No. Does it help? Yes, sometimes a lot. Failure is often followed by success. We owe it to ourselves to try.

It is important to know that thoughts often turn into beliefs. But neither thoughts nor beliefs are always facts. Repeat after me, "Thoughts and beliefs are not always facts!" We do not have to believe what we think. To choose healthy thoughts begins with becoming aware of our thoughts. Of course, you may think you already know what you think. But, in fact, we think thousands of thoughts every day and we are not aware of many of them. That's why we have to pay attention to both our thoughts and feelings because we can't change them if we don't know what they are.

The good news is that we can successfully change negative or dysfunctional thoughts if we are willing to look at them, become aware of them, and make the effort to change them. And this can help us improve our relationships, take better care of ourselves, feel happier, be more successful, and much more. It is said that a positive outlook—or positive thoughts—on growing old increases our lifespans by approximately seven years! Just becoming aware of how we feel about aging, for example, can either increase our stress levels or lighten our mood. Even our beliefs about death and dying, which are actually thoughts and feelings about death and dying, can be changed from feelings of fear to feelings of acceptance. Our thoughts can make a difference in how we experience anger, loss, regret, love, sadness, stress, happiness, shame, and other emotions that life circumstances trigger.

Here is another example: "I do not like my new neighbor." This is a negative thought that interferes with your relationship with your neighbor. This kind of thinking usually does not feel good. Here is a realistic thought: "I admit that I don't really know my neighbor. It is possible that I have jumped to a faulty conclusion. I will make an effort to get to know her." Notice how your feelings and even your behavior has changed just by changing your thoughts.

So, how do we choose healthy thoughts over distorted, unhealthy ones? There is a tool called Cognitive Behavioral Therapy, or CBT, that can be very helpful. There is a lot of science behind CBT that shows that this behavioral therapy really does work. You can use it with a therapist or you can do it yourself: on the bus, in your home, under a tree, just about anywhere. I invite you to go online for more information about CBT as well as examples of good books on this subject.

As we continue to walk down the corridors of aging, many of us will feel a painful sense of loss of family, friends, physical strength, dreams as well as our sense of self, of who we once were. As time propels us forward and closer to the closing of our own lives, I remind myself that whatever pain or loss enters my life, the way I think about it can soften this common reality.

As our own unique experience of aging continues, we learn that we must also let go of some, if not all, of our unfinished dreams since time is not on our side. But we can still dream new dreams. We really can! We can embrace the next expression of who we are becoming. We continue to adjust to waning physical stamina and the loss of the independence we once cherished.

But we are never out of choices as to how we think and feel

about these changes. Courage and acceptance come to mind for this late life task as we adjust to our unique and changing circumstances. We have choices here as well.

Every stage of life from childhood to Elderhood is an opportunity to grow, not just physically but mentally, emotionally, and spiritually. Growth is rarely easy but it is valuable enough to embrace and pursue. Try resisting some aspect of this new and changing experience of growing older like, for example, a new limitation. How does this limitation feel? How does your behavior change with this feeling? What are your thoughts about growing older? How do your feelings change when you have these thoughts? When you resist (a behavior) what happens to your thoughts and feelings? You actually do have the power to change your thoughts, feelings, and behavior no matter how old you are.

Life at this stage is as unique as the stages we grew through when we were younger. It is a time of uncertainty. It can feel like a slide into the unknown. Will I be afraid? Will I die slowly? Will I die alone? Will I suffer too much? Or, will I be one of the lucky few who simply goes to sleep one night and never wakes up? We might feel a loss of control over our lives. Sometimes we feel afraid. We can't always change what is happening but we still have the power to change how we experience what is happening to us by changing how we think about it. Medications can help. Meditation can also help. Diversion from our discomfort to something special and pleasant can help even if that diversion only exists in our minds. Take a virtual trip to the beach in your mind. Fly among the stars. Use your mind to visit loved ones. Go anywhere, any time, to wherever or whatever brings you pleasure, relief, rest, peacefulness, etc. This mental diversion can actually affect how you think and feel. I invite you to try it!

We don't have a lot of choice as to how this chapter closes, but we do have some choice as to how we experience it. Will we deny what is happening? Should we reject it? Can we accept our waning time on earth? Acceptance does not mean that we welcome this limited time, or that we like it. It simply means that we recognize the truth of whatever our inevitable path looks like and adjust our thoughts to make it as comfortable as possible.

We do get to choose how we ride this last wave. We always get to choose. Hopefully, we have learned that happiness does not happen because we have pursued and found it. Pleasure is something we can pursue and find, at least temporarily. But true happiness happens as a by-product of how we live our lives at all stages and what choices we make along the way which includes our thoughts, feelings, and behaviors. As Jack Kornfield wrote:

> "Like a sandcastle all is temporary.
> Build it, tend it, enjoy it.
> And when the time comes
> Let it go."[31]

Are we accepting of what is before us during the fading autumn of our lives? Do we accept the inevitable or do we deny it or rage against our fading time on earth? Some of us will choose to deny what is before us during our last days. Some of us will rage against it. Some of us will reject the obvious. Some of us will let go and slide softly into the night of a new experience. Who can say what is best for us as we leave what we have always known? That's the hard part: leaving the laughter, tears, sunshine, favorite foods, trees, love and loss, memories, loved ones, and even pain. Arriving into our human families during birth was not easy and leaving is sometimes not easy either. Helpful advice for the journey is important but there is no judgment about how we make that journey. We have all had a personal experience of what we call life. When our time is up, we have to leave, ready or not. As we leave let's remember to check our wings.

# VOICES FROM THE FRONT

# What Does It Feel Like To Grow Old?

"I feel the dependency and loneliness of growing old."

Irene 85

"I try to cope with the difficulties of growing old by simply not thinking about it. I also keep busy and read good books."

Helen 90

"Growing old is OK with me but not with my body."

Anonymous 80

"There will be times when you will become very depressed and you will find that happens around the corner. All the things you will go through cannot be avoided but going through personal things makes you stronger and you appreciate life more. Whenever I felt down, I felt I was able to cope with it because I believed there was always tomorrow and this is part of my journey."

Taylor 69

"As I have experienced it, life becomes more difficult with each passing year. I lost my freedom to drive and gradually my independence. Especially difficult was selling my house. I have counseled my friends of my generation to stay in their homes as long as possible to avoid being warehoused in a senior center for independent living. Yes, I am bitter about the way American culture treats old people. I lived 20 years in France and observed all generations living together. I never saw a senior center throughout my entire time in Europe. Old people were not considered a problem for their children or grandchildren to solve by stashing them away."

Anne 88

"If I only knew what lies beyond death, I wouldn't be so afraid."

Anonymous 90

"I am thoroughly enjoying my old age. I have had a fine life and I am particularly grateful for our family. Our children and grandchildren are exceptionally good people who have never given us a single problem. I didn't expect to live to this great age, but now that I'm experiencing it, I hope to live a few more years. Death doesn't frighten me and I plan to sleep peacefully in my grave forever more."

Muffy 90

"When my friend reached 102, she shared her deep sadness with me. 'I have not talked to a person in two weeks, she said, and whenever someone comes to sit down with me, I feel they come to sit with the phenomenon of a 102 year old woman not really to converse with ME. The chatter is superficial and boring.' "

Kiki 66

"I have been diagnosed with early stage Alzheimer's disease. I do not want to be kept alive and a burden on my family when I no longer know who I am or who my family is. Because of my diagnosis, my autonomy to make an informed decision on my own behalf is taken away. This is cruel. Why is it that many western cultures support euthanasia for animals who are suffering and/or dying but that support is limited and complicated when it comes to human beings?  Something is very wrong here."

Vinnie 79

"I hate growing old. I hate losing my looks. I hate losing my energy. But I love my tranquility, no stress."

Laura 89

"There are several ways I keep myself stimulated. I drag myself to Piedmont Avenue on my walker or in my wheelchair. You should see me use my wheelchair!"

Flossie 91

"I am envious of those who say they are enjoying taking courses, discovering new venues and find joy in every new day they are alive. I love to paint and work with wood but to what end? Who needs what I might build? Who wants my paintings? Like my knowledge and passion towards career work, they are products of my past. In my today's world they will sit on no one's shelf and gather only dust in my mind."

Dudley 81

"I'm not an American old person but a senior citizen of this planet. I have surprised myself by referring to myself as an old person without feeling humiliated lately. I am 68 in May and it still feels like a big joke on the inside. I feel 38! For me my greatest need is to feel useful and have a sense of purpose. And I feel I am accomplishing this wish by supporting my children and their children."

Diane 68

"Both of my parents gave me one of the greatest gifts of my life. They helped me to overcome fear of death and dying. They both faced death with such courage and engagement, that I learned that Death can actually be a beautiful, though painful experience. The key is to embrace the whole process, not resist it, and share it with others as you do. I want this to be like that on my death bed. I want to still be in a position to be a force of light in this world, even as I begin to embrace the light in the next."

Robert 62

"I use to think I had to buy a lot of cosmetic products to look good on the outside. The more years, the more products. Hooray for the day I finally learned that our beauty resides on the inside."

Sally 76

"Will I have the courage to end my life when I no longer have a satisfying life?"

Anonymous 83

"Am I really invisible?"

Anonymous 69

"BE GRATEFUL! Count your lessons and share them with others and live life generously. It is a blessing to the one who gives. Reach out to those less fortunate than yourself and do what you can to help. When I am asked how I am doing, my answer is often, 'Better than I deserve.'"

Loren 84

"So far, I have felt that the 70's is an adventure, another kind of travel. So, I can be said to have yet to fully discover my old age. And this summer has brought one bodily misadventure after another, so that my project during these months has been to solve as many maladies as possible and then take stock. But thoughts about death are with us all along. My late husband felt from an early age that it would be terrible to miss the moment of one's own death. After all, it was one of the two most significant events of one's life. It was not to just be slept through. (And he was glad to get his wish. It was not quick. In the end he said his last months had been a great time.) I hope I will feel this at my own end. In response to two friends who tended to demand much of the world as if their due, he demonstrated the cheer of the pessimist by saying he woke each morning with a sense of triumph. I'm alive, I'm intact, I'm sane! What more could one ask?"

Karma 76

Why are we here? What's it all about? Think of all the life challenges and bodily struggles and a lifetime of creating bonds and experiencing love; only to be snuffed out for forever?

Jamie 70

"When I was turning fifty I felt like I was turning into an old man, and I set out to do something about that. I began working out in earnest. I took a yoga class. I joined a competitive men's softball team. I started to work on lowering my cholesterol. Throughout my fifties I remained very active. The year I turned sixty I became beset with a series of health issues. Beginning with hearing loss due to a brain tumor. The tumor eventually went away and since I could no longer play baseball I took up walking with earnest. I try to walk almost four miles a day. I guess my biggest fear is becoming irrelevant."

Peter 62

"We all die alone. I'm not afraid of death, but I am afraid of dying."

Abe 97

"If our bodies and minds hold out we can experience the liberation we have waited for much too long. Knowing that our end is coming closer triggers anxiety and that anxiety can be a motor to do what you always wanted to do and never dared to. The feeling of not having to lose so much anymore: beauty, sex appeal, and a reputation all can be left behind in earlier chapters of life. A new freedom calls out to us."

Kiki 66

"Life is like a soap bubble. It's duration depends on how you blow it. Once it bursts, it is gone. Disappeared. Enjoy this moment."

Mehdi 84

"I am 75 years old and I have to say that some parts of being older are fantastic! I know myself very well and am more self-accepting than ever before. The physical issues are somewhat challenging, but that is more than offset by the freedom to choose my daily activities and to structure my life according to my own preferences. I spend less time trying to impress others and more time by myself. I love my independence and enjoy being my own company, conversely, what time I do spend with others is of a higher quality, though of less quantity. I am blessed with enough income to take care of myself and to help others. I am also blessed with a keen mind and a fantastic sense of humor. Not a day passes that I do not laugh out loud. I have had a rich life and look forward to many more interesting experiences. I learn new things every day and I see things with new perspectives all the time. I have few regrets and much, much gratitude for all the blessings I have received. I wish I had better mobility, but I'm still vertical and able to take care of myself. I have a deep faith in life and in love and the rewards that come with working hard and living an honest, authentic life. I hope I have many good years left. I still have so much to learn and to do."

Glenda Lynne 75

"I'm afraid to go to sleep at night because I might not wake up in the morning."

Anonymous 84

"In my youth my fingers once ran over the piano keys with grace. Now, in my old age, my fingers walk with hesitations and stops."

Dolores 88

"Life grabs ahold of you. I experience life more seriously in everything I do and I am learning more. Growing old is not about death and dying even though each day brings me closer to death."

Bobby 69

"Dying is just another thing which has to be accepted. I am 83 and loving my life. I am more tolerant now than I was at 50. I accept more easily the nastier things that happen. Today I have been told that my original cancer is back. Dismayed, I am not, in fact I am looking forward to beating it. At 59 I would possibly not be so tolerant. Most people fight this and become obsessed with the disease. To me it's just another mountain I must climb and I will. Life becomes more valuable as you get older which makes the fight more worthwhile. My ethos is a smile. It keeps me and those I meet happier and more at ease with whatever the world gives us. Just smile and you will feel better."

Robert 83

———— ✳ ————

"It takes so much time to take care of the body. I do not like this loss of time."

Janet 75

———— ✳ ————

"Aging feels scary. It also feels liberating. Life is short. Make the best of it. Be friendly with the moment! You will be glad you did."

Joretta 81

———— ✳ ————

"I know I look old on the outside but I feel young on the inside. I like it!"

Anonymous 80

———— ✳ ————

"I'm afraid to die alone."

Jane 79

———— ✳ ————

"I am old but when I drink whisky and dance I am always young."

Pricilla 78

———— ✳ ————

"I don't notice growing old until I get into situations and I think, 'How did I get here? Why am I at the end of the hall?' I kind of forget I am old until I forget things."

Shirley 90

"What does it feel like to grow older? Scary, Joyous, Challenging, Exhilarating, Frustrating, Smug, Innocent, Daunting... but basically it feels like a birthday every single day I'm alive."

Laura 73

Around my 70<sup>th</sup> birthday I recommended a novel *Water for Elephants*. After reading it I wanted to run back in time to live happy ties and correct sad ones. One thing is clear—you can't change your past Life, even old events good or bad and we really do change a lot as we age. What we do have is time - the future. The question is how do we spend it? And with whom? Before any major pain or illness, I've looked at life through 40 year-old eyes with no real thought of dying or the 'end.' My wife and I are Catholic but many times question the church, the doctrine, the hierarchy and abuses of power. And I have the universal question, 'What's on the other side?' What really happens when we die? The answer to me is, 'I don't know, we can't know because that transition is as amazingly different as coming into this world. We come into this life alone and we leave alone. All the people, thoughts and material things are forfeited to the unknown. So now what? Do all the people around me have an eclectic past they would like to go back to? I think I'll begin to ask and see what happens."

Peter 81

"If you've got your health, you've got it made...so goes the saying, I think, but no matter the wording, it's true. I never imagined that by my late 60's I would be unable to walk or that I would have lost my husband. Just as one denies ever really getting old I denied ever getting sick or being alone. But you know what... it's all okay because I've been lucky in that I have a wonderful family and friends, and enough money to fight this illness and provide a very nice roof over my head. Life, even an old, sick one, is good. I mean, as another saying goes, "What's the alternative?"

Lynne 73

"I have had a lot of loss (husband and family) and I am blind. But I am still here and I can think and express myself. I can't believe how lucky I am."

Olga 88

"I no longer care much what others think of me. There are few benefits in growing older, and this was one. I just don't care."

Leo 87

"Aging has been an interesting experience. Sometimes good, sometimes not so good. Trying to focus on the good is very helpful but there are some areas of regret. My biggest one being when you have always been able to say 'yes' to different activities, new experiences, volunteering, etc., then you find you must say 'no.' Not because of lack of interest but because of just being physically unable. I find this very difficult but I will continue to do as much as I am able and try to appreciate what I can do."

Denise 82

Steven Richards the poet said, "When we age we shed many skins: ego, arrogance, dominance, pessimism, rudeness, selfishness, uncaring … Wow, it's good to be old!" I agree, it is actually easier to be nice when we age.

DDL 84

"I think for a woman, the hardest thing about growing old is becoming invisible. There's something very front and center about being young. Unfortunately, being visible is more difficult as we age."

Amy 80

# CHAPTER 4

# ACCEPTING THE UNACCEPTABLE, OR NOT

*"Footfalls echo in the memory,*
*Down the passage we did not take,*
*toward the door we never opened,*
*into the rose garden."*

T.S. Eliot
*Four Quartets*

AN DEATH BE a gift? I believe it can. Thanks to the work of Frank Ostaseki, co-founder of the Zen Hospice Project in northern California, many people have learned that death can be an important friend. Frank has sat at the bedside of more than 2,000 men, women, and children as they lay dying. He has been a wise and benevolent guide to those who are making their final passage through life as well as to those who have read his book or heard him speak. In his recently published book, *The Five Invitations*, he brings to life a reality few of us know and is a sought-after speaker to many different organizations including the medical profession. He is a rare and authentic authority on the subject of death and dying.

Thanks to Frank's profound and sensitive work with the dying, I am learning to be comfortable with an awareness of "death" sitting gently nearby. This awareness or idea of death is truly a gift because it reminds me and us to be more aware of life, to marvel at life, to be grateful for life, and to live life more fully. Without the awareness of death lingering close by, I would forget that my days are numbered and, like most people, would simply take my days for granted. Instead, I am nudged into remembering to treasure each day.

An occasional focus on the awareness of death quietly sitting nearby really does help us to embrace this inevitable closing of our lives with more grace than struggle. For me, death sits quietly and softly on my right shoulder. Too much of the time I still forget that death is always lurking. The price I pay for this blind spot is that day by day my life continues and I do not remember that each day is a gift.

Too much of life unlived follows too many of us to our graves. An unlived life is often spent by watching too much TV, spending too much time in bed, isolating ourselves from social and family contacts, drinking too much alcohol, smoking too many cigarettes, spending too much time online and not being engaged in life. All of these can be normal distractions but when overused they subtract important pieces from a meaningful life. So, it is a real loss when I forget to remember that the awareness of death can enhance my moments and your moments, day after day. Awareness of death is a gift waiting for our embrace. When we forget to treasure each day, and I often do, we lose the opportunity to savor all that life has in store for us.

But accept death and the dying process? Why would anyone want to accept the process of dying, especially when it can sometimes be painful, prolonged, undignified, and frightening, and we are helpless to stop it. Some believe that holding on tight and hanging in there are signs of great strength. However, according to Chuck Palahniuk there are times when it "takes much more strength to know when to accept an unwelcome truth and then to let go and do it."[32] Although difficult—sometimes very difficult—acceptance of what feels like the unacceptable can make the unacceptable more like a form of soft surrender, and less like a battle or struggle against defeat when victory is not possible.

Please do not misunderstand. It takes courage to open ourselves to accept what we do not want. This is certainly true for me. And yet our choices are limited: we can resist reality, deny reality, fight reality, or we can open our hearts and minds and even our bodies to the truth that will eventually loom before each of us. "We are never out of choices, no matter how desperate the circumstances."[33] We can always choose what we think.

As I write these lines, I wonder what my eventual inevitable death will look like. Will I be afraid? Will I die slowly or suddenly? Will I be ready to die? Will I be ready to say goodbye to loved ones? Will I leave a broken relationship without trying to heal it? Will I cross over into something better? Will I die alone? Will I suffer? Will my family suffer? I cannot know. We cannot know.

It makes sense to fight for something as long as there is a reason to hope that what we want is achievable, even if only part of what we have prayed for is possible. There is reason to hope or to fight for a new cancer cure. There is reason to hope and to fight for a benevolent change in a relationship. But there is no reason to hope or fight for a return to youth when you are more than 80 years old, like I am. Old age can be eased and enhanced by our lifestyles but we can't stop it. We can only resist or accept this universal truth of growing old and dying. Don't forget that birds do it, fleas do it, animals and trees do it, and friends and family do it, too. All creation is born and all creation must die. As part of creation we must too.

It does make sense to fight for something, even relatively small things, when positive change or healing is possible. When it is not, we have to acknowledge that fighting can work against us. Denial does not make it go away or change what might feel like an awful and painful truth and yet we all must eventually face death and the dying process. It is the heart and mind that resists, fights, and denies uncomfortable realities. It is the heart and mind that hangs on and won't let go. It is also the heart and mind that chooses acceptance. Denial does not make death go away or change the way our journey feels. But acceptance of what is real and true can make a big relaxing breath possible and soften the reality we all must eventually face.

Acceptance of death, or anything else, does not mean that we agree with what we are facing. It only means that we are willing to receive the truth of what is before us, or what is required of us in a given situation. Death is an inevitable truth—a universal reality. That's all. Nothing more. Accepting this truth softens this lurking reality that life ends for all of us.

We actually die a thousand small deaths during the unfolding of our lives as a necessary process of growth and change. The body dies, the heart dies, and the mind dies—over and over. Pain, sorrow, fear, confusion, regret, desperation, and loneliness accompany us on our journey. Gratitude and forgiveness also live here. However, the time comes when we have to lay our body down for one last time. If we try to hang on, we extend our departure time but we don't stop our journey. Eventually the time comes when we must cross over the threshold of life into the mystery that lies beyond.

Remember that death and dying reflect an inevitable and natural transition into the last chapter of our individual stories. For most of us, fear and anxiety are common at this stage. We cannot know what dying or death will feel like. We can only know that we will suffer losses and, in time, we will no longer be among all that we have known and loved.

It is true that any unknown can feel scary, especially if we are alone. Change itself can feel threatening. For all of us this final stage is the gradual closing of our life cycle without a map to guide us or an explanation of what is happening to us. We cannot know what the dying process will be for us or even the course of this final transition as it is happening. We can resist it, deny it, or fight it or, we can take a deep breath and accept what is happening and what will eventually come to pass. Difficult? Yes! But it is true. "What we run from stays with us longer. When we fight, we only make it stronger."[34]

When we actually open and accept dying and death, the fear of death often dissolves or at least diminishes. There is something about staring death in the face that seems to shatter the fear because knowledge and understanding of death issues can actually reduce the fear. Once gone, the fear might return and we will have to face it again and again but now we know how to do it. Once we make friends with death, there is the possibility of feeling peace about leaving here and arriving there. We want that. I certainly do. However, the great mystery decides.

Time marches on, and we are eventually left with a choice to deny the unwanted changes that come with old age or illness, fight against these changes, or accept and make peace with what is. Remember that each of us is a unique and unfolding personal story. Aging and death are simply part of our unique story and our personal journey.

If we reflect on all the numerous stages of our lives, we will notice the anxiety that accompanied so many of our experiences of not knowing. Can you see that we have actually been practicing the discomfort of not knowing for most of our lives, including, for example: waiting for the news about a new and very important job interview, a college admissions test that will determine our future, diagnosis of an illness, etc. This is the normal and common anxiety of not knowing what will happen. So, there are ways that we have been experiencing the discomfort of not knowing for most of lives. And, we survived! We have done it before and we can do it again.

Even in my discomfort of change and not knowing, I am committed to letting go as best I can when letting go is the wisest and the best thing to do. I need to prepare and practice the art of letting go. I must accept aging and death. It is truly often the best option in most situations. However, I do not know with certainty at this time if I will make the appropriate choice for myself when my turn comes. I can only hope I will have the courage to face whatever truth looms before me. I need to prepare and maybe practice the act of letting go for myself since I often grasp and hold on to things in my everyday life. Hopefully, my commitment to acceptance and letting go at this time will make it easier to accept the inevitable when it arrives. And, arrive it will—for each and every one of us—ready or not. I want to be ready.

At this stage of our lives many questions arise. We need a detailed plan of action for approaching the end of life and dealing with illness, living wills, the process of burial, comfort when we are hurting, how to talk to medical doctors, etc. All manner of things! I know of no more useful book on this subject than *A Beginner's Guide to the End: Practical Advice for Living Life and Facing Death*. I bought a copy of this book for all my children as well as for myself. Truly this is an important book and a must read for the dying and for those who love and care for them. Grateful hats off to BJ Miller, MD and Shoshana Berger for writing this extraordinarily helpful book.

Remember, age is measured not only in chronological years but also in terms of our mental health, our living conditions, finances, and both physical and emotional support. These are all major factors that influence the experience of aging at all stages and ages. We age differently and for different reasons and having a plan that considers these various aspects of end of life can be invaluable.

Each of us is going to be old no matter how hard we fight or how hard we resist the universality of aging, dying, and death. Each of us, if we are fortunate enough to live a long life, will age.

The famous stages taught by Elizabeth Kübler Ross are relevant here. Dr. Ross taught us that when the dying process is near, we go through five stages, more or less, in this order: Denial, Anger, Bargaining, Depression, Acceptance.[35] The following examples are mine:

- Denial: "I am not dying."
- Anger: "This is not fair. The doctors are to blame."
- Bargaining: "I will serve you forever, my Lord, if you heal me. I will apologize to everyone I have hurt."
- Depression: "I don't want to live. Life is too hard. No one cares about me."
- Acceptance: "I am ready. I can let go. I have no choice but I believe that there is something that awaits me after death."

As a palliative or comfort-only caregiver, Bronnie Ware spent many years giving comfort care to the dying and says that: "People grow a lot when they are faced with their mortality. Some changes were phenomenal. Each person experienced a variety of emotions, as expected…yet every single patient found peace before departing. Every one of them."[36] According to Ware, the most common regrets are these:

- "I wish I'd had the courage to live a life true to myself, not the life others expected of me."
- "I wish I didn't work so hard."
- "I wish I'd had the courage to express my feelings."
- "I wish I had stayed in touch with my friends."
- "I wish that I had let myself be happier."

It is my understanding that Ware gave her special comfort care to people whose basic needs were taken care of. They had homes, sufficient food, clothing, and friends and family. Our final journey might look very, very different if we die alone, or in poverty or without medical care. Mother Teresa has made that point very clear. We need a Mother Teresa in America.

I would like to add some important questions I once read by Jack Kornfield, a beloved Buddhist teacher and clinical psychologist. He distills all the important issues we feel on our death beds with this:

"How well have I loved?
How well have I been loved?
How fully did I live?
How deeply did I go?"[37]

Can you imagine yourself, as you lay dying, asking

yourself these questions? These questions will certainly be the questions I will be asking myself. However, when we die alone and without sufficient food, clothing, and shelter, I doubt if we will ask ourselves any of these questions. One usually does not philosophize on an empty stomach!

Growing old sometimes involves coming to terms with mistakes, regrets, loss, missed opportunities, loneliness, painful and unfinished family relationships, and medical problems. Rejecting or denying the pain, the fear, sorrow, anger, etc., often keeps these difficult life events alive at some level, even unconsciously, and they can follow us on to our death beds. As they say, "What you resist persists." It is especially difficult if our struggles are unspoken and not shared with another.

David Kessler, MD, a well-known authority on the physical and emotional aspects of dying, has written about the importance of meeting the special and specific needs of persons who are living out the last chapter in their lives. Based on his many years of experience with patients who were dying at home, in a hospital, hospice, skilled nursing facility, etc., he came to know what the dying need from us. Kessler lists sixteen special and important needs that dying people expressed in his book entitled, *The Needs of the Dying*.[38] The following represents a shortened list from his book:

1. Honest answers to questions.
2. Freedom from physical pain.
3. The ability to express personal feelings and emotions about pain.
4. An understanding of the process of death.

5. The chance to die in peace and dignity.

6. To not die alone.

7. Respect for the body after death.

I could not recommend Dr. Kessler's book with more enthusiasm and gratitude. It goes a long way toward educating us on what dying people want, need, and should have in an enlightened and caring environment. His book is highly recommended by hospice and other palliative (comfort) care organizations. The knowledge of these needs is a gift to the dying as well as to those who love them and are caring for them. Remember the day will come when we will all experience similar needs. I hope and pray that all of us will be fortunate enough to have these basic human needs met.

At this waning time in our lives we often benefit from help. We need a partner, mother, father, child, priest and or pastor, friend, or sibling who can simply hear us. Our words, our regrets, our love, our grief, our fear, our gratitude must be heard by a listening heart without judgment. A cool hand on a hot brow can express care, concern, love. Thoughts, feelings, memories, and personal stories can be powerful. To be alone with a difficult and unspoken secret can be very painful. Holding secrets inside ourselves can keep us from healing. When I even think about exposing my secrets to the sunlight, I can feel my body tighten with resistance. What to do? Hopefully I will have the courage to open to my own secrets. But not all secrets benefit from the light of day. Some secrets express their healing power in darkness. Think carefully as to how you choose to share or not share your personal thoughts and feelings. Be courageous but wise.

A caring heart that holds no judgment is a special gift to someone who is walking the final walk. The awareness and acceptance of our inner truths, no matter how difficult, is like a wide opening of one's arms to what is in front of us. It's like facing something straight on instead of turning our backs on it. Because acceptance is not always easy at first, it is important to know that it is a process that usually happens over time; a confession to oneself or another. It can take time for our burden to take flight. But, oh what a blessing acceptance can be! It's like the heart and mind sighing in relief together. It's like a simple surrendering to the truth with compassionate understanding. It can be said that it feels like a great big relaxing ahhhh.

Forgiveness is often a part of this acceptance when we recognize and take responsibility for an error we have made toward another person or toward ourselves. Over my eighty plus years here on earth there are many ways that I have hurt or harmed others: my children, my friends, my family, the storekeeper on the corner, the neighbor across the street, the man on the bus. Many of you will relate to this. I cringe when I remember. My heart feels shame. It is true that I often did so unknowingly. However, I am still responsible. No matter that my actions were often simply small and insensitive acts, the effects of these acts could have caused unseen distress. Our pain, fear, anger, ignorance, or confusion can distort what we see, what we feel, and what we do not feel. Forgiveness, mistakes, and resistance are all parts of being human.

Similar to the somewhat rocky path to acceptance, forgiveness also frees us from ourselves. It is a process that Wikipedia defines as, "…to pardon someone (including ourselves) even if that someone is unrepentant. To forgive is to excuse a mistake or an offense. It does not mean that you agree with or even like the offender. It only means that you love even though you do not like. In sum, forgive and forget."

Forgiveness is also a process that often takes time but oh, the freedom. Mark Twain said, "Forgiveness is the fragrance that the violet sheds on the heel that has crushed it." Ahh, to be able to forgive like that violet. I'm going to have to work on that one.

The good news is that you and I get to make choices. It might be one of the most difficult choices of our lives but we can choose to deny, resist, or surrender—and accept reality. This choice often involves an internal struggle. "I will! I won't! I can! I can't!" The struggle can be life-long, and this might be the first time we have ever considered opening our hearts and minds and letting go. It doesn't matter. The struggle is real and usually not easy. Acceptance might be difficult at first but so much easier and worthwhile when we open our hearts and minds to whatever is before us. I invite you to consider this when you can; if you can.

We die in different places: in hospitals, at home, in hospice, or a nursing home. Some people die in the forest, some die in the streets. But the majority of us want to die at home. Unfortunately, approximately eighty-five percent of us end up dying in a hospital. However, if we die at home or in a medical facility, and we are receiving loving care and companionship, we have a chance of having the needs described by Kessler met. We can and should ask to have these important needs met. Ask loud and clear and over and over if necessary. Having someone who can advocate on our behalf may be necessary. We have the right to be as free of pain as is possible. We have the right to a nonjudgmental heart and ear that will listen to you and hear what you need. We have the right to be treated with respect and kindness no matter your medical condition. Period!

Yes, I know it can seem more comfortable to cling to denial and reject what is before us. That choice is up to you. In many ways, this denial is a normal response to an extreme situation like dying. But we have to choose. We still get to deny that we are dying. We can still try to fight the inevitable. No one can make this decision for us and there is no wrong decision. There is only our personal choice. What is right for us might be wrong for someone else. It doesn't matter. It is our right to make this decision without judgment from ourselves or others. Of course, caring advice, helpful advice, and or medical advice is also ours to choose or reject. No one walks in your shoes or mine. Living can be too hard right now. Some might even say that dying is easier. Maybe I would rather die.

What about hope? Can't I hope for what I want? Absolutely! Hope has its place any time that there is even the smallest reason to believe that what one wants might just be possible. If staying alive longer to attend a special event is what you truly want, having hope can sometimes make that happen. Hope can also soften whatever unwanted experience we are having. Make friends with hope. Hope plays an important place in the closing of our lives. But eventually there comes a time when it is in our self-interest to choose to accept the indisputable fact that our individual stories are ending. It is time to let go.

I once thought that my father might have scared himself to death. But he died quickly, so he probably had a clot in his lungs that was unknown to everyone in our family. We will never know. My father was in the hospital and had just been diagnosed with a cancer that would kill him in about two months. My sister Denise and I were with him in the hospital. I explained the diagnosis to him and the time he had remaining. Denise had been a nurse and she and her physician husband told our dad that they were going to take him home with them and make sure that he did not suffer. But when Denise and I arrived at his hospital room the next morning, we knew immediately that he was already on his final journey. At some level, he had made a choice and it was the right one for him. Because hearing is usually the last of our senses to fail, I immediately crawled into his hospital bed, held his right hand, and talked directly into his right ear. I told him that if he could hear me, to squeeze my hand. I repeated this over and over and over but he never squeezed my hand. So, for the next hour and a half, we talked to him as he walked to the end of his time on this earth: "Look for the Light, Dad. Look straight ahead. No need to look back anymore. Look toward the Light." And then, he took his final breath and crossed over. He was gone. We knew not where, but he believed in the heaven of his heart.

Think on the following words from Ira Byock, MD, paliative care physician and author. These words can help us as we say "farewell" before, during, and after death:

"Please forgive me."
"I forgive you."
"Thank you."
"I love you."

What about life after death? There is and always has been a universal longing to know. I would like to know. I know you would too. What we do know is that with death the body falls away and some believe the fall is into nothingness. Many say that the spirit is then free to fly, to become another possibility of the numerous possibilities that might be available to us in an After Life.

Many people believe that something wondrous awaits us as long as we have tried to keep the beliefs of our various religions. If we have not, some form of punishment might await us. There are also religions that embrace the belief that after we die, we are reincarnated into a new human life here on earth. Our lives have no beginning and no end as we move from one life to the next. This new life is usually related to our behavior in our former life, or perhaps lives, and can provide opportunities to learn more about love, compassion, forgiveness, and consciousness. Other religions simply lack the moral concepts that are said to dictate much of our experience after death. Some of these beliefs state that we are essentially forms of energy and that this energy, upon death, is transformed into another form of energy. We know not when, what, or how.

The following are just a few of the many women and men who have thought and struggled and meditated on the answer to this deeply important issue of what happens after we die.

Carl Jung: Famous psychologist who studied many great religions and concluded that, "All great religions hold out the promise of a life beyond, of a supra-mundane goal which makes it possible for mortal man to live the second half of life with as much purpose and aim as the first." Dr. Jung's famous studies point to hope for a reason.

Albert Einstein: Famous physicist who tells us that energy cannot be created or destroyed. Many believe that Spirit is a special form of this energy and is considered by many to be a force that animates all living things.

Ram Dass: Famous psychologist and spiritual teacher who tells us that the secret of death is that, "We are infinite. We do not die." The end is not the end. More reason to hope and let go of fear.

Dr. Serene Jones: President of the Union Theological Seminary in New York tells us that, "There was a time when we were not and there is a time when we will not be again."

Rabindranath Tagore: Bengali poet who says, "Death is not extinguishing the light; it is only putting out the lamp because the dawn has come."

Louis Pasteur: Famous chemist and founder of microbiology and immunology, said, "A little science distances you from God, but a lot of science brings you nearer to God."

Old Bible Testament, Ecclesiastes Chapter 3: "To everything there is a season and a time to every purpose under the heavens: a time to be born and a time to die."

In sum we can't know, not really. We can only fall back on our own religious, spiritual, philosophical, or personal beliefs. What we can know is that things do eventually fall apart. Nothing, absolutely nothing, lasts forever—not your heart, not your job, not your children, not your house, not even your beliefs! Given this reality we might want to consider a quote from Sabrina Newby who tells us,

"Don't be afraid.

Change is such a beautiful thing,

said the Butterfly."[39]

# INFORMAL NOTES

## INTRODUCTION

1.  Population Reference Bureau
2.  Gene D. Cohen, MD. Geriatric Psychiatrist. *The Mature Mind: The Positive Power of the Aging Brain, The Brain in Human Aging*

## Chapter 1. THE JOURNEY BEGINS

3.  Gordon Livingston, MD. Geriatric Psychiatrist. Too Soon Old, Too Late Smart
4.  Laura Carstensen, PhD. Psychologist and Stanford researcher on Aging
5.  AARP (AARP American Association of Retired persons). Solace In Alcohol and Drugs. October 2017
6.  Helen Fields. Smithsonian Magazine 2012
7.  Karl Pillemer. Smithsonian Magazine July 2012
8.  Robert Samuelson. Washington Post. December 2014
9.  Laura Carstensen, PhD. Psychologist and Stanford Researcher on Aging
10. Robert Samuelson. The Happiness Curve. The Washington Post

## Chapter 2. CAN YOU SEE ME NOW?

11. Gordon Livingston, MD. Geriatric Psychiatrist Too Soon Old, Too Late Smart
12. Michelle Barnhart. News and Research Communications
13. Brague Deacon PhD. Social Psychologist. Applied Social Psychology 2011
14. AARP Bulletin (American Association of Retired Person). Age Based Discrimination 2013
15. Jonny Ball. English Television Personality
16. Ashton Applewhite. *This Chair Rocks*
17. Drs. Karin Ouchida and Mark Lachs. "How Ageism in Healthcare is Affecting Society" February 17, 2019. American Society on Aging 2019
18. Ibid.,
19. Ibid.,
20. Ralph Waldo Emerson

## Chapter 3. THE ROAD WELL TRAVELED

21. Ralph Waldo Emerson
22. Founder of Dynamic Aging Institute
23. Jack Riemer. *Finding God in Unexpected Places*
24. Mark Cooper and James Selman. The Eldering Institute
25. AARP Foundation (American Association of Retired Persons) Housing Issues
26. William Butler Yeats. "The Second Coming"
27. Pastor Gregory Rapp. First Methodist Church, Hanover, Pennsylvania
28. Helen Keller. Deaf and blind political activist and author 1880-1968
29. Dr. Verne Wheelwright. Personal Futures Network
30. American Psychological Association

31.  Jack Kornfield, PhD, Clinical Psychologist, Buddhist Teacher and co-founder of Spirit Rock Meditation Center. *Path With a Heart*

## Chapter 4. ACCEPTING THE UNACCEPTABLE, OR NOT

32.  Chuck Palahniuk. 100 Best Palahniuk Quotes
33.  Gordon Livingston MD. Geriatric Psychiatrist. *Too Soon Old, Too Late Smart*
34.  Chuck Palahniuk. 100 Best Palahniuk Quotes
35.  *On Death and Dying*
36.  *The Top Five Regrets of the Dying*
37.  Jack Kornfield. Clinical Psychologist, Buddhist Teacher, Co-founder of Spirit Rock Meditation Center
38.  David Kessler, MD. *The Needs of the Dying*
39.  Sabrina Newby Quotes

# ABOUT THE AUTHOR

Dr. Livingston worked as a clinical and forensic psychologist for several decades. During that time, she taught at several universities and had a private practice in clinical psychology for adults. She also worked with convicted felons at a maximum-security prison hospital. At sixty-seven, she retired and then traveled to the mountains of Chiapas, Mexico where she spent almost 10 years working with Maya Indians. She is the mother of three, the grandmother of six, the great grandmother of two, and the guardian of one beloved cat.

*Without the loving support of Cary, Denise, Saydee, and especially Lisa, this book would not have seen the light of day.*

Printed in the United States
by Baker & Taylor Publisher Services